To Helena
Best m...
Larryan Jose

A BESTIARY OF BRIDGE

A BESTIARY OF

BRIDGE

James J. Kilpatrick

ILLUSTRATIONS BY LEE LORENZ

ANDREWS, McMEEL & PARKER

A UNIVERSAL PRESS SYNDICATE AFFILIATE

Kansas City • New York

Library of Congress Cataloging-in-Publication Data
Kilpatrick, James Jackson, 1920-
    A bestiary of bridge.

    1. Contract bridge—Anecdotes, facetiae, satire,
etc. I. Title.
PN6231.C615K5   1986   795.41'5'0207   86-17206
ISBN 0-8362-7930-1

CONTENTS

The Culbertson System

Systemnaticus Culbertsoni

MORE than sixty years have passed since the Culbertson System emerged from the primeval swamps of auction bridge to be crowned king of the world of contract. Observe in the Plate opposite, if you will, the jaded eye, the haughty proboscis, the commanding torso. In the same way that we speak of a polo player's polo player, or an actor's actor, this was a beast's beast. Many systems have come and gone since the reign of this lordly creature, but none has had a greater impact upon the game as it popularly is played.*

In the period of its prime, roughly from the appearance of the Blue Book in 1930 to the rise of Charles Goren's point count in the early forties, the Culbertson System ruled supreme. Like a colossus it bestrode its vast domain. It fed on side games and rich stakes.†

---

*Well, maybe Charles Goren has had as great an impact. Hard to say.

†That's a pun, pal. We writers often have pun pals.

The great beast's finest hour came in January 1932. Some months earlier Ely Culbertson had wearied of the criticism his system was getting from Sidney Lenz and other competing experts who were busily promoting their "Official System." Culbertson was a superb showman. He was also a linguist, gambler, author, lecturer, world traveler, chain smoker, and self-made intellectual. The New York Sun described him as "that perpetual exhibition of skyrockets and roman candles."

He challenged Lenz to what would be hailed as the Bridge Battle of the Century. Culbertson would put up $5,000, Lenz $1,000. They would play 150 rubbers, half of them at the Chatham Hotel, half at the Waldorf Astoria, both wagers to go to the New York Infirmary for Women and Children. Lenz accepted—he scarcely could refuse—and after months of haggling over details play began December 7, 1931, at the Chatham. Culbertson played 88 rubbers with his wife Josephine, 62 with other partners. Lenz began with Oswald Jacoby, but the two experts could not get along. After 103 rubbers Jacoby withdrew: "Our ideas about bridge were so radically different that it would be unfair for me to reenter the match." Lenz finished with Winfield Liggett. Alfred Gruenther, who twenty years later would command NATO forces in Europe, served as referee. Millions of American bridge lovers followed the matches play by play. After the first 27 rubbers, Lenz and Jacoby were ahead by 7,030 points, but this was their high mark. By the time play moved to the

Waldorf after Christmas, the Culbertsons were ahead by 17,000 points.

The battle was unbelievably close. Twenty-five hands were passed out; 854 were played. The Culbertson team held 1,745 aces, the Lenz team 1,771. The Culbertsons held 1,775 kings, the Lenz team 1,741. Their honor points were virtually identical—3,649.5 to 3,648. It was skill and stamina (and some crushing doubles) that carried the Culbertson System to victory by a margin of less than 9,000 points—122,925 to 113,945. The Culbertsons won 195 games and 77 rubbers, the Lenz team 186 games and 73 rubbers.

Toward the end of the thirties, Culbertson lost interest in his creature. It slowly became an endangered species. Today the habitat of the purebred Culbertson System is thought to be confined to the Every Tuesday Club of Tulsa, Oklahoma, and to the tables of the Ladies Sodality of Saginaw, Michigan.

The Revoke

Movus Dumbus

NOTHING good can be said of the Revoke. It appears rarely; it is held in universal disdain; it always shows up at an inopportune moment when it significantly affects the play of a hand. The Revoke also is known as the Renege, in the same fashion that woodchucks are known as groundhogs and the partridge is known as the quail. It lives in underground dens, where it sometimes hides behind another card, sometimes in the midst of a suit of the same color. The Revoke may be identified most readily by its tearful eye and by the long tail that perpetually lies between its legs. The fur is generally a blush red.

On discovery, its cry is a combination of a growl, a howl, a moan, and a groan. Unspeakable expletives are not unknown. The animal's cry of distress at once is followed by an opponent's call for "Director!" Heads turn. Lips curl. The Revoke slips away, often taking a trick or two in its pouch, and returns to its lair to join its companion, the Insufficient Bid, in the shadowy copse where the Irregularity dwells.

5

The Preemptive Bid

Panthera Leo Ignavus

F E W beasts of the contract jungle are more familiar, but less understood, than the Preemptive Bid. It is something like a lion, but not exactly like a lion. Outwardly it is bold, daring, fearless. Inwardly it is weak, devious, sneaky. The Preempt is amazingly swift. It pounces into the auction, often in third position, at the slightest hint of hesitation on the part of its enemy.

Usually it is found in the well-protected forests of non-vulnerability, less often in the exposed savannahs where "down two" is no bargain. The character of the Preempt is not altogether admirable,* for the beast is essentially greedy. There is a shifty element at work. As it springs into action, its whole purpose is to prevent the opposition from having any fun by finding a certain game of its own. This defensive leap is not to be confused with the Jump Shift, which is something else entirely, and not really shifty at all.

---

*But it certainly is more admirable than the character of the Psychic Bid, which it in no way resembles.

The Jacoby Transfer

Transferus Jacobi

FIRST identified in Sweden in 1953, though under a different name, the Jacoby Transfer appeared in the United States in 1956. Its discoverer, Oswald Jacoby, described the creature's principal features and undoubted virtues in an article in *Bridge World,* and before long it became established throughout the land.

Other transfer companies occupy a more limited habitat. The Rubin Transfer, for example, operates only through opening bids of four clubs, four diamonds, or four no trump—a circumstance calculated to intimidate the opposition. The Morris Transfer, a part of the International Precision System, is used chiefly to transfer people whose last name is Morris. It is the Jacoby Transfer that enjoys the widest customer satisfaction.

You will notice in the Plate opposite both the powerful musculature of this friendly beast and also its deceptive eye. After an opening of one no trump, the opener's partner may respond with a transfer bid of two hearts. Does this mean strength in hearts? Say not so. It means strength in *spades,* an interesting fact that may elude the inattentive opponent who has failed to check the declarer's card.

The object of this complex maneuver is to coax a bid of two spades from the opener, so that eventually the contract may be played in spades with most of the strength concealed in declarer's hand. It seems a lot of trouble, but when one has a chance to move one's furniture from a poor neighborhood to a better neighborhood, it's nice to call the moving van.

Like any common carrier of freight, the Jacoby Transfer will haul any old trump contract it is asked to haul, but to deliver a club contract by a response of two spades is to risk damage in transit to the merchandise. Inexperienced players especially will want to treat the beast with prudence. It eats amateurs and forgetful partners without the slightest compunction, but given proper respect, it's a great steer.

The Life Master

Dominus pro Vita

B EHOLD the vivid plumage! Behold the regal eye! As they say of the California condor and the great horned owl, there is no mistaking the Life Master. This handsome bird feeds on anything—open pairs, master pairs, zip Swiss, flighted knockouts—on anything involving three other birds and fifty-two cards.

Interestingly, the call of the male is different from the call of the female; he will be heard late at night in a low repetitive call of *toppord, toppord, toppord,* which sounds amazingly like *top board, top board, top board.* Her call is a musically accented cry of *GO-poyns, GO-poyns, GO-poyns,* which is understood to mean *gold points, gold points, gold points.* *

The Life Master first was observed in 1936, when ten of these magnificent creatures were identified. Among them

---

* For an interesting and authoritative description of bridge calls, see "Sounds of the Jungle," by Robert Fitzwater Robertson, doctoral dissertation, Indiana University, 1957. Unpublished.

were such well-remembered specimens as Oswald Jacoby, Howard Schenken, Waldemar von Zedtwitz, P. Hal Sims, and B. Jay Becker. Charles Goren was sighted in 1938, Helen Sobel Smith in 1941. Ornithologists attached to the American Contract Bridge League believe the youngest Life Master on record is Doug Hsieh, who in 1981 reached that level at the tender age of eleven years, ten months and four days.

Most of these brilliant birds come early to the rank of Junior Master (*D. studius*), advance to Life Master in their aggressive thirties, mellow slightly in their forties, tend to an avuncular molting past sixty, but never lose their triumphant eye. They are equally adept when nesting north–south or east–west. Their phenomenal memories enable them to recall every successful hand they ever played. Their recollection of disastrous sets is not quite so acute.

The Redouble

Duplices Gemini

T HE first observation to be made about the Redouble is that in the heyday of auction bridge, Redoubles were commonplace. The rules then permitted unlimited Redoubles, with no daily bag limit, a temptation that appealed to young men and old gamblers. Today the Redouble is rarely observed. The creature emerges from the Reckless Forests, breathing fire and baring fangs. It is indiscriminate in its choice of prey. It will devour declarers as avidly as it devours defenders. The cry of "redouble!" is at once a challenge and an insult.

The story is told of a high-stakes game in Dallas in which Wallace Whifflebee, sitting south, vulnerable, fell to bidding spades with what may best be described as wild abandon. His wife Bessie provided indications of mild support. The Sydney Simmses, sitting east–west, kept stubbornly in pursuit of hearts. The auction climbed to four spades from Bessie, five hearts from Sally Simms, five spades from Wally, pass from Sydney, pass from Bessie, and double from Sally. Throwing discretion to the winds, Wally *redoubled.*

It was then that he discovered, to his considerable dismay, that somehow he had failed properly to sort his cards. Two clubs had wandered into a small grove of spades and had taken cover. What he firmly believed to be a seven-card spade suit with a hundred honors was in fact a five-card spade suit with the king missing. The king was in Sally's hand, along with four other trumps, and the hand was down five. This was in May of 1939. Bessie Whifflebee spoke not one word to her husband until August of 1945. She was reading the paper at breakfast. "The war's over," she said. He broke into sobs and the pair was tentatively reunited.

Redoubles should be approached with extreme caution. They are always dangerous.

The Dummy

Equus Asinus Silens

WHAT can be said of the Dummy? Not much, in point of fact, for this docile beast has almost nothing to say for itself. No particular talent is required to become a Dummy. None is required to serve as Dummy. In Party Bridge, as distinguished from Duplicate Bridge, the Dummy may be excused from the table altogether, whether to dump the ashtrays or to powder its nose.*

During the play of a hand, the Dummy ordinarily may voice but a single sound: "Failing?" This must be uttered in a neutral tone, rising slightly but politely to an interrogatory level on the second syllable. Proper Dummies do not say "failing?" in a way that suggests that declarer may actually be revoking; such a breach of form may evoke a glare that conveys an unspoken response meaning "Of course I'm out, you ass!"

Well-bred Dummies do not touch their cards until instructed to touch them. They do not voice editorial opinions by frown, by sniff, or by eyebrow. A Dummy never has much fun, but at least it doesn't get yelled at.

---

*Dummies may be excused for any reason. The next Dummy you see, ask it to open the window to let some smoke out.

The Squeeze
Lampropeltis Classicus

T HE most interesting thing about the Squeeze is its infinite variety. The editors of the Official Encyclopedia of Bridge have identified at least thirty-seven Squeezes, among them the Vise Squeeze,[1] the Alternative Squeeze,[2] the Backwash Squeeze,[3] the Hedgehog Squeeze,[4] the Barco Triple-Double Squeeze,[5] the Compound Squeeze,[6] the Crisscross Squeeze,[7] the Hexagon Squeeze,[8] the Jettison Squeeze,[9] the Pseudo-Squeeze,[10] the Submarine Squeeze,[11] the Suicide Squeeze,[12] Bonney's Squeeze,[13] Shroeder's Squeeze,[14] and

---

[1] L. Visus Hurtus Likus Hellus

[2] L. Alternatus variegati (for zinnias, *see* p. 14).

[3] L. dorsolavi (nice for two, in a hot shower).

[4] L. terraporcinus

[5] L. trio duo Barci (up the wrong arboris).

[6] L. compressio complexus daily

[7] L. L. transitus transversos (used mainly by surveyors).

[8] L. octowhoopsis

[9] L. heavo-hocus pocus, dominocus

[10] L. phonus bolognus non est lampropeltis

[11] L. subaqua, meatballa

[12] L. morituri te salutamus

[13] L. Bonneyi

[14] L. Shroederis

Winkle's Squeeze.[15] Isn't that *enough*?

The most familiar Squeeze is the Simple Squeeze. Here the menacing reptile wraps its helpless victim in the coils of a damaging discard. The victim struggles. Should he let go a naked ace? Should he hold a protected queen? His cries of anguish are to no avail. "I have been squeezed," the victim mutters, or, if he would embrace the verb form as it once was employed by President Reagan, "I have been squoze."[16]

Whether one has been squeezed or squoze, it is a most frustrating experience, for one feels all the pain of a plump rabbit in the coils of a boa constrictor. This is by no means a comfortable experience—the coils are often cold and usually clammy—but it is a familiar experience.

When the play of such a hand has ended, it is considered good form for the victim to say to declarer, "Nice Squeeze!" The proper response is *gesundheit*.

---

[15] L. Winklorum

[16] Presidential Documents, Vol. 21, No. 32, p. 14, Aug. 5, 1985.

The False Discard

Et Tu Brute

T HE fields and forests of Bridge are inhabited by many creatures whose principal characteristic lies in their capacity for deception. The art of dissimulation, it may fairly be said, is indeed their long suit. Among these are the Negative Double, * the Psychic Bid,† and most deceitfully, the False Discard.

It should be emphasized that the False Discards are in no way related to the Impropriety.‡ Not at all. They are not even third cousins once removed. The False Card lives by sham, by pretense, even by fraud, but this is honest sham and honorable pretense, and perfectly legitimate fraud.

The False Discard comes in various colorations, high, low, and medium rare. It is found in tripletons as well as in doubletons. Observers report that the False Discard is held in

---

* Which see, p. 96

†You might look at this one, too, p. 59

‡It is not related to the Irregularity either. As a matter of fact, the False Discard has only a few first cousins. They live in Boise. An uncle lives in Sioux Falls.

greatest affection by lawyers and by gynecologists; it is highly regarded by insurance agents and by members of Kappa Alpha fraternity also. Journalists, because of their dedication to the Pursuit of Truth, almost never employ a False Discard.§

For purposes of identification, one should look for eyes that are innocent but studious, and for gestures that are at once indifferent and regretful. The visage of the False Discard is marked by a look that expresses the inevitability of ill fortune. It is as if to say, "Farewell, my queen!" Under which is the guarded jack.

The prudent observer, suspecting something fishy, would be advised to recall that Shakespearean sonnet which begins, "O! Never say that I was false of heart." The lady sitting east may well be false of spades.

------

§If you will believe this, you will believe anything.

The Slowpoke

Testudinida Tarda

I N the census of 1920, approximately 2 million Slowpokes were counted at Bridge tables of the United States and Canada.* In the ensuing decades their population has grown steadily, though not dramatically, and authorities predict a stable level of perhaps 3 million in the twenty-first century.

The Slowpoke cannot be mistaken for anything else. Its hard shell is totally impervious to murmurs of impatience. The firmly compressed mouth, the astigmatic eye, the tentative phalanges—all these mark this studiously deliberate beast. Will the Slowpoke bid? Yes, but not until its hand has been sorted, resorted, opened, closed, opened again, breasted, chested, counted and recounted, and thoughtfully appraised. "Pass," says the Slowpoke at last, thus opening the auction. The Slowpoke is looking at one naked ace and two red jacks. Such difficult bids plainly require a great deal of time.

---

*Except in the Yukon, which was not surveyed.

During play the Slowpoke is as careful. A contract in no trump best demonstrates the characteristics of the species, for here we typically observe the half-drawn discard, the replaced card, the half-drawn alternative selection, the replaced alternative selection, the closing and opening of the hand, the counting and recounting of tricks here and tricks there, the troubled sigh, the upward gaze.

One healthy and mature Slowpoke can drive a Tournament Director to strong drink. The Slowpoke can goad the most accommodating partner to cries of "Come *on,* Josephine!" or "Clarence, it's *your* bid!" Such exhortations leave the Slowpoke unmoved. Its trance may even be prolonged by interruptions. You will understand that the Slowpoke has many natural enemies, but it has outwaited every one.

The Alert

Lepus Curiosos

T HE circumstances under which an Alert may be examined are perhaps best explained by homely example. Let us suppose that Pat is sitting south and Mike is sitting north. Pierre is sitting west and Jean is sitting east.

Pat and Mike have played together a long time. The two Hibernians are bold, aggressive, innovative. For them the Standard American System holds no appeal. Precision bidding, as it usually is defined, strikes them as slovenly. They have therefore devised between themselves some entirely new bids, carefully tailored for the most bizarre exigencies.

Pat opens one club. Jean passes. Mike then bids two diamonds. This is not, as you might innocently surmise, a Jump Shift. Not at all. This is a part of the Sword, Axe & Eyeball Convention that our inventors have contrived. Under the rules, Pat is now bound to turn to Pierre, sitting on his right, and to say, "Alert!"

Pierre may then, if he chooses, say, "Expliquez, mon ami, s'il vous plaît," or simply, "Whassat mean?" Pat is obliged to

♣

◇

say: "A jump shift at the one level to a suit of the opposite color denotes a hand holding at least seven points but not more than nine, with distribution of four/four/four/one, in which the singleton is the king with the green and yellow sword."

"Oh," says Pierre.

While this colloquy is continuing, Mike is suffering terrible pangs of remorse and apprehension, for he has *completely forgotten* the agreed-upon response to one club in their Sword, Axe & Eyeball Convention. In fact he is holding twenty-two points, including six hearts with a hundred honors, the doubleton ace/king of spades, the one-eyed king with the axe behind his head, and the queen who holds the flowers in her fist. His proper response was two *spades,* denoting great strength in the suit just below spades, but under no circumstances, by groan or grimace or a dropping of the jaw, may Mike suggest that a misunderstanding has occurred.

As it happened, because Pat had opened with only eleven points and five squat clubs, the hand was played at two diamonds and Pat waxed exceedingly wroth.

Such is the perverse nature of the Alert. Sometimes it clarifies; sometimes it confuses. Sometimes it leads to cries of "Director!" Sometimes it leads to a plenary session of the executive committee. In the melancholy case at hand, the Alert launched an evening in which Mike never again held more than four points, including the two-eyed jacks and the queen with the flowers on her wrist.

The Forgetful Bidder

Memoria Obliviosa

THE Forgetful Bidder (FB) sometimes is confused with the Slowpoke, but the two species are in fact quite distinct. The problem with the turtle-backed Slowpoke is that it concentrates too much; the problem with the slothful Forgetful Bidder is that it does not concentrate enough.

An immature FB ordinarily waits until a simple auction has been completed, e.g., one heart/four hearts. "I'm sorry," the FB apologizes, "but may I review the bidding?" The more mature FB goes into a trance the moment a hand is dealt.* At the second round the FB snaps to awareness: "Where are we?" "Did you bid two spades?" Late in life, and especially late

---

* Cadwallader believes that childhood experiences weigh heavily in the development of mature Forgetful Bidders. The fourth-grade pupil who regularly forgets his lunch, and the seventeen-year-old girl who persistently forgets when it is time to come home—these are Forgetful Bidders in the bud. See "Advanced Analysis of the Weak Two in Southern California," Joseph X. Cadwallader, University of Tijuana Press, 1981, Vol. II, p. 182 *et seq.* It is only fair to acknowledge that Parsons strongly disagrees. See "Early Evening Overcalls," Frances Fitzhugh Parsons, Pont Neuf Press, 1984.

in the evening, the FB *cannot remember even its own bids.*

Some observers hold that the Forgetful Bidder is also, in almost every instance, subject to other lapses. The FB cannot remember trumps, it cannot remember whether the lead is on the board or in its hand, it cannot recall—despite the most arduous and laborious thought—whether the lonesome nine in the Dummy is good for a trick.

Our own researches tend to confirm these observations. In one instance, reported by Tigerman in his invaluable monograph† a case is described involving a Forgetful Bidder in Palm Beach. Playing one night at the Breakers, the FB forgot that he was playing with his wife and went home with an attractive neighbor.‡ On such rocks are partnerships regrettably broken.

---

†Bo Tigerman, Hur man kan vinna bridge utan att förlora vänner. Bonfer Publik, L.T., Stockholm, 1961.

‡See *Holpenschlock* v. *Holpenschlock,* 118 So. 2d 918 (1934). *Held*: In light of "intensely provocative circumstances," award of generous alimony is not excessive.

The Finesse

Via Vulpis

I N the Kingdom of Bridge, some creatures live a highly protected life. The ace of trumps, for example, is never in danger of being devoured. In a no-trump contract, the lead of *any* ace will survive a predatory foe. Of other species, such as singleton kings, it may fairly be said that sometimes they are in danger and sometimes not. It depends.

The Finesse, pictured in typical action on the facing page, is almost always in some degree of peril. Its sole function is to make its way from point A to point B without disaster striking. Sometimes the Finesse may be helped along by clues derived from the bidding. In these instances its task is not so filled with apprehension. If West during the auction has voiced nothing but the pass doleful, while East has been repeating its bids pugnacious, it is likely that the Finesse can travel from north to south in the first-class cabin, watching a movie and sipping free drinks. But not always, for the Finesse is in peril not only of good defense but also of bad luck. It is probable that West's only face card is the fateful honor.

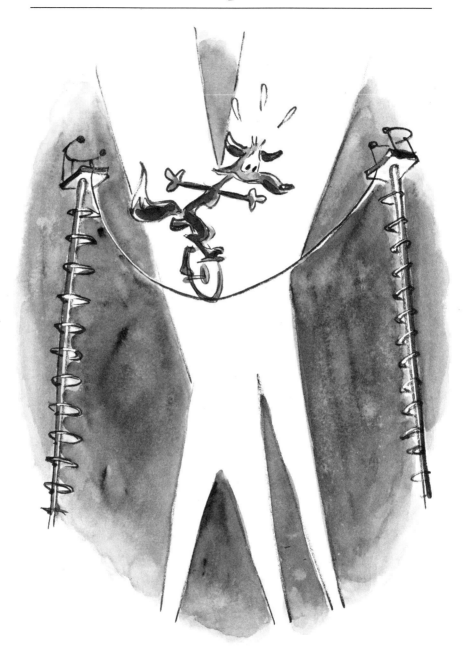

By nature the Finesse is reclusive.* It would rather not be put to work at all. It would prefer to stay in its den, reading a good book, hoping that progressively revealing discards will permit it to remain undisturbed. But the Finesse is a dutiful creature. When the telephone rings, and it is ordered to ride as a nine toward an ace/queen on the board, it will embark bravely on its errand. If it gets felled by a wrong-sided king, *tant pis*! The Finesse shakes off the dust, disdains the bruises, and prepares to ride, ride again.

---

*Its cousin, the Chinese Finesse, by contrast, is positively aggressive.

The Little Old Lady

Femina Parva Senecta Pasadenae

I T may as well be acknowledged in candor now, lest it be confessed in expiation later, that the Kingdom of Bridge is not inhabited wholly by creatures of honest mien and steadfastness of character, such as Goren's pure opening one no trump. There is a beast that can be relied upon always. Bridge also is a world of artful deceit.* In this regard, let us examine the Little Old Lady.

It should be said at the outset that this unassuming East, when one is sitting South, often appears in a guise that is not little and not old. She may have reached what the French call a certain age. She may have a considerable girth; she may be sylphlike. Often we observe good, solid, respectable glasses; sometimes we observe sunglasses. The accent may be New England or Midwestern. Most often there is some trace of Natchez. In every case, however, we find an unmistakable aura of innocence, inexperience, and a touching vulnerability. Lit-

---

*See, for example, the False Discard, p.23, and the Psychic Bid, p. 59.

tle Old Ladies do not say they are only beginners, nor do they inquire whether spades are higher than hearts, or vice versa, but they silently imply a need to be assisted along the way.

The temptation, until one has gained experience with Little Old Ladies, is to treat them with benign tolerance and to play them for two extra tricks. O reckless pigeon, be not deceived! The Little Old Lady who has been saying doubtfully, "Ah reckon Ah have to pa-yass," is the same Little Old Lady who will snap "double" when the bidding gets to a shaky four. The eyes, so veiled but a moment ago, suddenly are filled with fire. She makes the devastating lead. *Wham*! Cross-ruff! *Wham, wham*! Down two! "Ah decla-yare," she says prettily, "we cert'nly did get lucky on tha-yat one." Then she looks helplessly at the sco' card. "Tha-hat's five hundred for ouah side?" She knows perfectly well that down two vulnerable is five hundred for her side. "You men," she says, "have such fine heads for figures."

Of the first one hundred players to achieve the rank of Lifemaster, fourteen were women. Every one of them started as a Little Old Lady.

The Lead

Genesis Prima

THINK of sparrows, if you please. Or think of warblers. Think of caterpillars. The problem of beginning ornithologists and entomologists is to sort out the varieties, the sub-species so to speak, of sparrows, warblers, and those fuzzy little covered wagons that have such fun on an oak tree. There are so many of them.

So it is with The Lead. There is the Lead from Top of a Sequence. There is the Lead of the Lowest. There is also the Lead of the Highest. In the case of a singleton these two birds are indistinguishable. In the open meadows of No Trump we find the Lead of the Fourth Highest from the Longest and Strongest.

Some Leads, like cowbirds, are regarded as inferior Leads. Among these is the Lead Away from a King and the Lead of the Top of a Worthless Doubleton. Some Leads, like jaybirds and mockingbirds, make their presence instantly known. They cry out to be led. The call is *leadme, leadme,*

leadme. * Most Leads are not so readily identified; they are all equally unpromising.

Perhaps the most common Lead during the play of a hand is a Lead long ago identified with whist. This is the Lead through Strength or the Lead up to Weakness. During the 1920s many fledgling players learned this dubious rule along the highways: "When the board is on your right, lead the weakest thing in sight. Burma Shave."

The most common opening Lead has a crest like a punk rock hairdo, a covering of disorderly feathers, and a severe headache. This is the Desperation Lead or the Lead from Fright. It is a Lead to be avoided, but like the ubiquitous sparrow, it is a Lead that nests in every table in the land.

---

*Robertson, op cit., p. 12.

The Oldest Member

Senissimus, Summa cum Privilegio

T o speak of the beloved creature known as The Oldest Member of the Club is to speak with affection and admiration of The One Who Always Shows Up. Early to arrive, among the very last to leave, the OM is known primarily for its stamina, and for its astounding memory.

Our research has turned up an ageless OM who in 1986 could remember every detail of a Small Slam brought home in an Alabama regional in 1951. Six hearts, it was, vulnerable, doubled by Harry Hornsby on the strength of the trump ace and a guarded king, but Lucy Fothersby swindled him out of the king with a Simple Squeeze that was a work of classic perfection. The two later were unhappily married.

The Oldest Member rarely is the Club's best player, though it finishes often enough in the points to keep the creature in a benevolent mood. The OM sometimes is asked to function as a Tournament Director, but it is ill-suited to executive tasks. Neither is it a good choice to serve as Scorekeeper, for its gregarious nature makes it impossible for it to chat and to calculate all at the same time.

Old Members rarely retire. So long as they can hold a hand of Bridge, they will be found in their natural habitat. Eventually they move on to the Grand Bahama in the sky, where they play in open pairs into eternity.

The Cue Bid

Taurus Validus

IN the 1920s and 1930s, the Cue Bid seldom was seen or heard in the forests of Bridge. (It never was seen at all in the meadows or swamps). While not an endangered species, it once was as rare as the Psychic Bid, and it was much more useful. In this period, the Cue Bid used to charge abruptly, even truculently, from the woods. West would open one heart; North instantly would say two hearts. This served two purposes. First, it discomfited East, who had opened her mouth to make the very same bid; and second, it told South something interesting. The Cue Bid signaled first-round control, always an amiable prospect.

Thanks to careful herd management, commencing about 1937, Cue Bids grew in number and circumstance. They now abound throughout the auction. You may see them anywhere.* In the modest scope of this work, it is impossible to identify every sub-species, but mention should be made of the more familiar classifications of the Cue.†

---

*In some parts of northern Virginia, the Cue Bid has become a serious pest. It does great damage to apple trees and to trump contracts. Pennsylvania has a bag limit of two Cues a rubber or four a session.

†The most famous master of the Cue, Minnesota Fats, is best known for the eight ball in the side pocket.

There is, for example, the Light Takeout Cue Bid, which comes with lettuce and tomato. There is the Astro Cue Bid, which shows a two-suiter that will fit under the seat in front of you. A highly popular strain is the Modern (or rockcrushing) Cue Bid, which holds not only two suits but also a tennis racket and two pairs of ski boots. Less known, perhaps, but still of much interest, is the Michaels Cue,‡ by which North informs South, after West has opened a minor, that North has good holdings in both majors.

Among the more exotic forms is the Colorful Cue Bid, discovered by Dorothy Hayden Truscott. Imagine, if you will, an opening bid by North of one heart. East bids two hearts. Is this the simple, old-fashioned, original Cue Bid, indicating first-round control? Of course not, or Mrs. Truscott would not have claimed a new species. What, then, does the two-heart bid portend? One has to think. Ah! It means that East has promising holdings *in two unbid suits of the same color.* What could these be? Clubs and spades! Isn't that nifty? Won't it produce an Alert?

Experts no longer are much impressed by Cue Bids. They have seen hundreds of the things. Lesser mortals continue to regard the Cue Bid with awe, and rightly so. The Cue Bid usually speaks of singleton, void, or ace. It strongly suggests *control,* and like big Black Angus bulls, these are powerful, dangerous, and valuable beasts to have around.

---

‡Discovered and classified by Michael Michaels of Miami Beach.

The Standard American

Pons Accipitridae Americanae

THE Standard American can best be described in metaphors of food. In New England it is clam chowder and baked beans. In the Deep South it is grits and red-eye gravy. In Texas it is five-alarm chili. In Iowa it is corn on the cob. Everywhere it may be compared to steak, potatoes, and pie *à la mode.* Life Masters, Grand Masters, visiting Italians, and experts from Argentina may scorn this indigenous bird, but in Saturday night foursomes throughout the U.S.A., the Standard American reigns supreme.

What is it exactly? It is hard to say. It was born of Vanderbilt, nourished by Culbertson, pedigreed by Goren, and much cherished by Little Old Ladies.* Among its more prominent characteristics are the Strong Two, the 12–14 Point Opening Count, and the basic Stayman Response to an opening no trump bid.

---

*It also has been much cherished by ornithologists, native Americans, the Audubon Society, and the U.S. Postal Service.

In the Standard American we find nothing devious, nothing sly, nothing arcane or mysterious. The Standard American may be counted on: It will never open a four-card major. Its signals (when it remembers to signal) are of the utmost simplicity: high/low to show a doubleton. In the Standard American, the uninfluenced opening lead of a king *always* promises either the ace above or the queen below. Top of the sequence, that's the American lead! Fourth highest from longest and strongest!

This is the old reliable, the tried and true, the ever dependable, rent-paying, trustworthy permanent resident who remains after all the exotic guests have left. Standard American! The authors, if not the experts, salute you.

The Interference Bid
Licitatio Interrupta

THE Interference Bid has but one role in life. It is *to get in the way.* This is all it knows how to do. If South opens with one no trump, West may intrude with two clubs. This says nothing about West's point count; it says nothing at all about his clubs except that he has nothing in clubs to speak of.* West's whole idea is to prevent North from making a Stayman response of two clubs and thus beginning an orderly, uninterrupted parade down the field toward Game or Slam.

Interference Bids are comparatively rare.† They never are used by the Oldest Member and only infrequently are employed by the Little Old Lady.‡ Usually they are found in the relatively protected cover of nonvulnerability. In their clumsy way they can be remarkably shifty. The Interference Bid often gets in the way of its own partner, for partners cannot always tell if their mates are only funning around, or if they

---

*Therefore we will not speak of them.

†Room Service will do them medium well done if you ask.

‡The Forgetful Bidder can't remember to use them.

honestly hold a legitimate fistful of clubs.

The Interference Bid is widely known by its common name of the Nuisance Bid,§ but we have preferred to adhere to the classic nomenclature. The name of "Nuisance Bid" suggests something trivial, something easily brushed aside. Be not deceived. A rude, crude, hairy-chested Interference Bid may be compared to a 200-pound linebacker and a 300-pound tackle. They're often tough to get around.

---

§In southern Alabama it is known as Mr. Buttinski.

The Yarborough

Manus cum Nihilo

T H E story goes that the Yarborough was not so much discovered, but rather was exploited, by a nineteenth-cen-
tury English peer. This was the Rt. Hon. Marvin,* earl of
Yarborough, scion to a name and estate justly famous in the
history of England. Born in 1830, he was educated at Eton and
later at Cambridge, where he excelled in mathematics, botany,
and the flugelhorn. After some years as a civil engineer in
India, he returned to his ancestral manor in Kent. There he
spent his evenings factoring numbers and sipping old port. He
spent his weekends playing whist at the Sign of the Bull. He
never married.

One evening in his study the earl heard a peculiar sound
outside. He looked up from his mathematical tables. The
sound strangely combined a whimper, a sigh, and a groan. He
opened the front door to find a bedraggled beast on the

---

*Only funning. His first name could have been George.

56

threshold.† It was instantly apparent that this poor thing *held no card higher than a nine*. Lord Yarborough warmed the pitiful creature, offered it tens and jacks, even a tender queen, but the beast refused all further sustenance. It transpired that it is consigned forever to the pointless diet by which it is identified.

As their relationship grew, Lord Yarborough determined to find the degree of frequency, or rarity, of his forlorn friend. He discovered that the odds against holding his namesake are roughly 1,827 to one.‡ His lordship was no dummy.§ At the Bull and at his London club, he began wagering a thousand pounds to one that no such hand would be held in the evening's play. Soon his lordship acquired many pounds and he became, as Macaulay said of Chief Justice Impey, rich, quiet, and infamous.

---

†This was in November 1893. The Oxford English Dictionary cites a first usage of the Yarborough in 1900.

‡The odds against holding a hand with no card higher than a ten are only 274 to 1; no card higher than a jack, 52 to 1; and no card higher than a queen, 11 to 1. Yarborough knew what he was doing.

§He usually was Declarer.

The Psychic Bid

Causa Obscura

PSYCHICS have a bad name, and justifiably so. The verb *to psych* entered the English language about 1917 as a shorthand form of *to psychoanalyze*. A bit later it took on the color of intimidation: Joe Louis psyched-out his opponents.* Still later it acquired a gloss of self-confidence: Jimmy Connors psyched-up for his matches.† In 1931 Dorothy Rice Sims put a name to the frenzied creature depicted here. This is the Psychic Bid. What it is, is the loonybird.

But like many a real-world loony, occasionally a Psychic Bid achieves amazing success. The example is cited of an opening bid by Martin Cohn in the Vanderbilt Team matches of 1967 in Seattle. Cohn was sitting south, not vulnerable, holding seven clubs from the queen, the jack and two lousy spades, a singleton nine of diamonds, and a singleton four of hearts. *He opened three hearts.* Peter Leventritt, sitting west

---

*Of course he knocked them out too.

†Often he failed to psych-up enough.

59

with a twenty-two-point blockbuster, was so unnerved that he failed either to double or to overcall in no trump. Cohn played the hand at three hearts undoubled. He went down six, but at the other table five hearts, doubled, made six. Such triumphs of irrationality are the exception.

In the early 1930s, the sky was dark with Psychic Bids. They rivaled starlings and the passenger pigeons of yore. Everyone who ever had bluffed at poker wanted to try a little psych at Bridge. Wild contracts resulted. Husbands screamed at wives; wives screamed at husbands. The Psychic Bid that bamboozled the opposition served also to puzzle the partner. Players asked themselves, what does it mean? Means it what?

The waves of Psychics disappeared about 1934 as abruptly as they had arrived. A feeling took root that the things did more harm than good. They were *legal,* but they hung around with Improprieties. Not good form, you know. In recent years, tainted by the implicit disapproval of the Grand Masters, the Psychic Bid has become almost as rare as the pileated woodpecker, a gaudy relic of a fevered time.

The Vanderbilt Club

Baculum Vanderbilti

FEW conventions in Contract Bridge have enjoyed a longer life or presented a more distinguished pedigree than the Vanderbilt Club. This was one of the many inventions and contributions of Harold S. Vanderbilt (1884–1970), a great-grandson of the original Commodore Cornelius (1794–1877). It was the commodore who begat William Henry Vanderbilt, the railroad tycoon who gave to American industry an immortal exhortation: "The public be damned." William Henry Vanderbilt begat William Kissam Vanderbilt, who not only enhanced the family fortunes but also begat Harold Stirling Vanderbilt, who in turn begat Contract Bridge.

It happened in this fashion. In 1906, as a twenty-two-year-old fresh out of Harvard Law, Harold took up auction bridge and swiftly mastered the game. His father had profitably shed most of the family's railway holdings in 1903. Young Harold would become associated with the management of the New York Central, but his heart was in yachting—and in

Bridge. Harold's father died in 1920, leaving an estate of $54 million.* For the next fifty years Harold was free to live the good life.

He enjoyed auction, but he found certain aspects of the game in need of improvement. In auction, the idea was to reach a contract at the lowest possible level, because all tricks counted toward game. Various proposals for change had been advanced, but all had been rejected. On October 21, 1925, cruising from Los Angeles to Havana, Vanderbilt effectively invented Contract Bridge. He devised the major change, by which only bid-tricks may be counted toward game. He developed the concept of vulnerability. He provided a bonus for the Little Slam and the Grand Slam. He worked out a scoring system by which the rewards for making a tough hand may be roughly balanced by the penalties for going down. And he put all this into a Code of Laws. The gentleman was a genius, the best friend that Bridge has ever had.

His bequests to the game include the Vanderbilt Cup, and more to the point of this compendium, the venerable Vanderbilt Club. Its habitat is everywhere; and its elements are too well known to require scientific description.

----

*In those days that was real money.

The Irregularity

Goofus Minor

THREE hearts," says North.

"Three diamonds," says East.

"Insufficient bid!" cries South.

An Irregularity has just stumbled onto the board. The Irregularity, like the sparrow, the snail darter,* and the Southern Democrat, comes in a wide variety of forms. Following we see the Irregularity identified by Feinberg† as the Exposure of a Defender's Card in violation of Rule 49. This hapless defender accidentally has dropped a queen of hearts. The queen has become a Penalty Card, and Penalty Cards are embarrassing objects to have lying around in front of you.

No illustration adequately could depict the emotions that envelop a table when an Irregularity sits down in one's lap. People at adjoining tables try not to look, but they cannot help

---

Tennessee Valley Authority v. *Hill,* 437 U.S. 153, 197 (1978), Powell, J., dissenting.

†*Unregelmassigkeiten, die ich erfahren habe.* Von Wolfgang Feinberg, Dusseldorf,1968. *Die nackte Blosstellung einer Abwehrspielkarte,* p. 921.

looking. If the Irregularity is large, the Tournament Director may be summoned. There will be talk of appropriate penalties. There may be some conspicuous thumbing of the Laws of Duplicate Contract Bridge. Sanctions may be discussed. It will be asked if penalties have been waived. Meanwhile the Irregularity just sits there. And sits there. And sits there until the Director tells him it's time to go home.

The depressing thing about the Irregularity is that it is found over so wide a terrain. Feinberg's basic classifications embrace Irregularities of Auction and Irregularities of Play.‡ Among the more familiar breeds is the Inadvertent Call, a call that may be recalled provided it is recalled instantly, *without pause for thought.* Few Irregularities are deep thinkers. They almost never pause for thought.

Another common Irregularity is the Call (or Bid) Out of Rotation. At a game of party bridge in Trenton, New Jersey, early in 1961, Madge Kingledorf, sitting south, held twenty-eight miserable hands in a row. In her frustration, before she had even picked up her hand in deal twenty-eight, she cried "Pass!" This was a Pass Out of Rotation. It cost her dearly, for when Madge at last picked up her cards and looked at her cards, she was stunned to see twenty-six points looking back at her. Alas, West passed, North passed, East passed, and poor Madge was left bidless but not speechless. It is best to draw a curtain over the incident.

---

‡Op cit., 14.

A rare Irregularity is the Bid of More than Seven, covered by Chapter V, Part II, Section Five, Subsection 38 of the Laws of Duplicate Contract Bridge. It might be supposed that Law 38 would never be breached, but one evening at the Chalmondelay Club in Worcestershire, where a regional tournament was being held, Anthony Prew-Sussex, sitting south, won a fiercely contested auction. His opponents had been madly bidding diamonds, but the auction stopped with Tony's slightly shaky seven spades. West doubled.

Carlton Cabiniss, sitting east, thought to break the tension with a small joke. "Eight diamonds!" he pronounced. He had forgotten that the Prew-Sussexes have not been known to have a sense of humor since the early 1700s. Tony turned to West: "Lead a club," he commanded. The lead permitted him to ditch a diamond loser in the dummy, to take the trick with the jack, and to spread his hand. "Sic semper Cabiniss," he said, and entered the score.

Two observations remain. The Irregularity should never be confused with the Impropriety. An Irregularity may be viewed with regret, but an Impropriety may be viewed only with scorn. The second observation is that, for all the space devoted to it in the Laws, the occurrence of an Irregularity is truly occasional.

The Tournament Director

Caesar Contestis

T H E Tournament Director is not easily characterized, but it is not easily mistaken for anything else. Let us begin with the epidermis. Like the skin of the lordly hippopotamus, it is amazingly thick.[*] The Director's senses of sight and hearing are keen. Indeed, these have been favorably compared to the eyes of a hawk and to the ears of the white-tailed deer.[†] It is as patient as the lily pad frog, which will wait all evening for an Impropriety to wander by.

The most phenomenal characteristic is that of memory. A mature Tournament Director has committed to heart the Laws of Duplicate Contract Bridge. It can tell you, without looking, that North is dealer on Boards 1, 5, 9, and 13, and that East and West are vulnerable on Boards 3, 6, 9, and 16. These are the easy rules. It knows what to do about a missing card (Rule 14), a call out of rotation (Rule 28), an inadmissible double (Rule 36),

---

[*]A.L. Merriman, *Great Tournaments of the Western World,* Eniwotek Press, 1981, p.304.

[†]Ibid. Ibid three hearts. What do *you* bid?

and a lead out of turn (Part III, Section One, Rule 53). All told, the Laws include eighty-nine rules, many of them with multiple subsections. The Director is master of them all.

At the cry of "Director!" this impressive creature moves swiftly but quietly to the scene of distress. It listens gravely; it acts judiciously; it imposes penalties; it brooks no backtalk. Subject only to an Appeals Committee, the Director has all the powers of an old-fashioned monarch. It is often loved, but it is still more often respected.

The Tournament Director's habitat is limited. It dwells solely among the tables of duplicate tournaments, whether large or small, but within this realm the creature is supreme. It welcomes the stranger, consoles the loser, counsels the novice on matters of protocol, and sees that the soft drinks are cold. Directors live under great tension and few live to a great age as Directors. They have a way of retiring to become the Oldest Members of their clubs. Females of the species cannot easily be distinguished from the males. They are equally magisterial and equally ferocious when attacked by an Impropriety.

The Scorekeeper

Custodius Libri Numerorum

T H E Scorekeeper lives a hopeful life. It hopes that no one will post the score for East-West in the column reserved for North-South. The hope is always in vain. Some dumb North inevitably will make a botch of things. The result is that a top may be recorded where a bottom is required, or vice versa, or versa vice, it makes no difference. Such incidents are responsible for the furrowed brow, the flaring eye, the curled lip by which the Scorekeeper may be readily identified.

For all of its travails, the Scorekeeper lives a relatively happy and protected life. It expects nothing to go exactly right, and its expectations are regularly fulfilled. The Scorekeeper is almost as respected as the Tournament Director, for upon its accounting do master points depend. Thus people are nice to Scorekeepers, and do not interrupt them when they are adding half-points in their heads. Ordinarily mild-mannered, the Scorekeeper can become quite irritable when provoked by the necessity of continuing erasures on its chart. It is best to treat Scorekeepers with caution, and to offer them nothing stronger than beer and ham biscuits. Too many carbonated beverages will aggravate their natural tendency toward gastric ulcers and itching of the scalp.

The Kibitzer

In Humeros Tollere

THE Kibitzer ranges widely through Europe and North America. It has been sighted as far south in Africa as Cape Town and it is seen occasionally in the better clubs of Calcutta, Dublin, Bad Kissingen, and Goodenough Bay.* Appleby believes that males of the species are more prevalent than females, though why this should be so—if it is so—Appleby never tells us.† The Kibitzer reportedly takes its name from the German word for "green plover," which is *Grüner Regenfeifer,* but we believe it more likely that the correct derivation may be found in the German word for "lapwing," which is *der Kiebitz.* Lapwings and green plovers are very much alike, except in German.

The Kibitzer may be most easily identified by its long neck and by its rolling eyes. Its early evening call is a plaintive *may-I? may-I?,* ‡ which carries a rising note of apologetic

---

* That's in Papua.

†F.X. Appleby, *Six Hearts, Down Four,* Nag's Head Press, Algonquin, N.C., 1983, p. 211.

‡ Robertson, op cit., p. 418.

inquiry. The Kibitzer is asking if it may sit down and observe. Ordinarily Kibitzers, once they are thoroughly housebroken, make quite acceptable company. They are expected to keep their mouths firmly zipped during the auction and the play, and they are permitted to speak between hands only when spoken to. Occasionally they may be asked for their opinions on fine points involving avoidable Finesses or Hexagonal Squeezes, and when their opinions are rendered judicially, with proper regard for *stare decisis,*§ they are favorably received.

This is not to say that Kibitzers are always hospitably regarded. At a regional tournament in Grand Junction§§ some years ago, Paul and Margery Hefflewhite were pitted against their unfriendly neighbors, the Ralph Pollingers. Margery's loquacious Uncle Harry, an avid player, was kibitzing. Just as Paul played to the thirteenth trick, apparently down one in a tough heart contract, Uncle Harry spoke up. "Ralph," he said, though they were hardly on a first-name basis, "you revoked on the sixth trick." It was true, but when the Director was summoned, something quite unexpected occurred. Because attention to the Irregularity had been called "by a spectator for whose presence the nonoffending side was responsible," the penalty was waived and Uncle Harry was at once sent home to Chattanooga. Paul remained down one, and he and Margery had words about Uncle Harry. So it goes.

---

§Decisive stare; lordly gaze.

§§That's the one in Tennessee. Others are in Iowa, Michigan, and Colorado.

The Loving Couple

Paramator Maledictus

THE following dialogue was recorded by Whiteside at Swan Lake, Idaho, during the North Pacific regionals of 1947. Owing to flawed equipment, the sound is often scratchy and Whiteside does not defend the absolute accuracy of his transcription.* Nevertheless, the recording provides one of the best specimens of the Loving Couple that our research has turned up.

*   *   *

SHE: Beloved husband, you must have had some reason for opening with one club instead of one spade. Will you tell your lambykins what that reason might have been?

HE: Precious lambykins, I expected to show my six spades with a hundred honors a bit farther on in the auction. And now, dear heart, will you explain why you bid just two miserable clubs over my one club?

SHE: Sweetheart, I do not especially care for that tone in

---

*Whiteside, Alden, "My Side of the KBRG Story," Boise, pp. 27-31, et seq.

your voice, but as any idiot can see, two clubs was the only call I could make.

HE: Light of my life, any numbskull who had played the game but twice in her life would have responded with one no trump instead.

SHE: [static, garbled] would have made a jump overcall if you had any sense at all.

HE: Your [indistinct] mother must have taught you *something* about responses.

SHE: [static] mother out of this!

HE: I can't tell you, my sugarplum, how I long to keep your [garbled] mother out of—

SHE: Listen, you crumb, do you know what you can do with your lousy one-club opener? And your lousy hundred honors in spades? And your ace/king doubleton in diamonds? You can go to bed with them, because you're not . . . [static, end of recording].

* * *

According to an affidavit obtained from a Kibitzer during discovery in *Sneemar* v. *Sneemar,*† the following terms of affection were employed during the interlude between two hands played in South Richmond, Virginia, in 1961: *Darling, dearest, precious, lambypie, duckie, numbskull, ignoramus, knucklehead, stupid woman,* and *stubborn pigheaded jerk.*

---

†Case 61-981, Hustings Court, Part II.

The Swiss Team

Cohort Canorum Alpinorum

IT needs to be said of a Swiss Team that it is—well, Swiss. It is neutral. It will play East/West. It will play North/South. It will play against other East/Wests and other North/Souths. Such is the stamina of these sturdy beasts that they will play all day and all night. They never tire.

The breed is not remarkably ancient. It was first recorded at Cincinnati in 1967, but it swiftly developed great popularity. In 1970 the first North American Swiss Team scaled the peaks of the Portland national championships. Since then Swiss Teams have been in action almost everywhere.

Toward the end of the 1970s a trend developed toward a somewhat smaller breed known as the Zip Swiss. Here twenty-five boards typically are played in a series of five matches, with a strict limit of five minutes per board. Only the hardiest Teams survive, but it is through creatures of this kidney that the breed improves.

The Signal

Vexillum Semaphorum

IGNALS were first observed and classified by Heinz in
1752.* Over the next two decades he recorded fifty-
seven varieties, some of which subsequently became
extinct. They deserved to become extinct. Useless things!
Others have undergone mutations. Many Signals continue to
frustrate the sender and to baffle the receiver. When these
interesting creatures work, they work well; they take no vaca-
tions; they work overtime at regular time, and they require no
health and hospitalization insurance. But when they do not
work, they can royally muck things up.

On the facing page Professor Lorenz has chosen to illus-
trate the Lavinthal Discard, so named for its discoverer, Hy
Lavinthal (1894–1972) of Trenton, New Jersey. He found the
creature in the winter of 1933, wandering homeless between
Grovers Mill and Dutch Neck. He took it home and learned
that the discard of a low card calls for a return of the lower

---

*Heinz, Gustaf, *Die Essiggurke in der Mitte,* Salzburg, 1752.

ranking of the other two suits. A high card calls for the higher ranking. So it goes.

The Lavinthal Suit Preference Signal is related in some unknown degree of consanguinity to the Revolving Discard, a version bred in England many years ago. A low card calls for a lead of the suit below the suit in which the signal is given; a high card calls for the suit above. Thus the discard of a low club calls for a spade return. If you can't return a spade, return a borrowed book.

A much older signal is the Blue Peter, discovered in 1834 by Lord Henry William Bentinck (1804–1870). The name derives from a naval signal that is hoisted in harbor when a ship is ready to sail. Lord Henry, incidentally, was the fourth son of the fourth Duke of Portland, an old Oregon family.

The Blue Peter, ordinarily employed when a lead of trumps is desired, has yielded to the rather more definitive Signals codified by Helge Vinje. A high-low shows the hand has one suit with an even number of cards and three suits with an odd number of cards, but then a high-low can mean other things, too. It can signal length. It can be an echo or a come-on. It can be an invitation to come upstairs for a nightcap.

That is one of the many ailments to which the Signal regrettably is subject. It is often misunderstood. When an odd-numbered card is needed, an odd-numbered card is not available. It has gone to Philadelphia for the weekend. A "high" has a way of not being notably high, and a "low" may well be an eight. The Signal that is dispatched with such care—for example, the discard of a two followed by a seven—may look like a barnyard low-high. In truth it may be intended to show a sequence of 9-7-5-3-2, a not very likely bunch of coconuts.

The best advice we can offer is to treat Signals with tender loving care. Do not keep too many of them in the corral at one time. Go for the simple, hardy strains, and leave the more exotic breeds to opponents who may horribly confuse themselves in the process of putting them to work. One final word: Never signal by winking, by rubbing one's nose, by positioning a pencil, by lighting the wrong end of a cigarette, or by kicking one's partner under the table. That's no Signal. That's an Impropriety.

The Yakkity-Yak

Sermonis Loquatis Convivialis

IT is perhaps unfair to say that the Yakkity-Yak is as unwelcome in the Kingdom of Bridge as a bull calf at a dairy farm, but it is not *very* unfair. The Yakkity-Yak has the voice of a crow, or of a wild goose, or of a tobacco auctioneer. Both the male and the female can be heard across a crowded room. Indeed, it is impossible not to hear the Yakkity-Yak in full cry.

These are the characteristics by which Yakkity-Yaks are most easily identified: The female of the species (less often the male) will be carrying pictures of grandchildren. There will be from four to seven grandchildren, and each of them is *darling*. The male ordinarily will be found to have a second avocation in golf (less often in bowling, rugby, or downhill skiing), and this he will introduce at almost any point. Merriman quotes from a party game in Phoenix:*

---

*Merriman, A.L., *The Fauna of Southern Arizona,* Tombstone University Press, 1974.

"Did you say two hearts? Right. Look, on the fourth green, I was short by about twelve feet, and was just lining up my putt—ah, two spades. Yes, I'll bid two spades if I never see the back of my neck. I was lining it up when this strange bird got between me and the cup and I was stymied. You pass, partner? That the best you can do? And I asked my caddy what was that dumb bird, and he says it's a kind of—ah, three hearts, eh—a kind of parrot or macaw. Three hearts, you say. It had the damndest red and green tailfeathers you ever saw. Three hearts, hunh. Okay, I pass. That bird took its own sweet time about getting across the green, I can tell you. I'm leading the king of spades, partner, and let's see what they have on the board. . . ."

The Yakkity-Yak may be found over a wide range of the United States and Europe. Its feeding habits are of no particular interest—potato chips and onion dip, crackers and cheese for the female, pretzels and peanuts for the male. Now and then, regrettably, the male and the female marry. They can be shut up, briefly, by offering shrimp to the male and caviar to the female, but this is an expensive way to buy quiet. The most effective treatment of the Yakkity Yak lies in a good pair of earmuffs.

The Professional
Partner

Gladiator Certificus

A MONG the relatively rare species in the Kingdom of Bridge—though it is by no means endangered—is the Professional Partner. Its habitat is limited. No record has been found of a Professional Partner in the duplicate woods of Walla Walla. None ever has been seen in Des Moines. But in the dense thickets of major regionals, where rich fruits are waiting to be plucked from the Gold Point Tree, the Professional Partner lurks.

The creature is not easily recognized. Let us suppose that you and your regular partner are playing in a sanctioned regional tournament in Wilkes-Barre. Because you have played in Pennsylvania bridge for some years, you are acquainted with the Life Masters most often observed in the area. Then you move to a table occupied by a Little Old Lady and a stranger who is at once sinister and disarming. Nothing about the stranger suggests anything untoward. *This is a Pro-*

fessional Partner. It is clad in a conventional sports coat and conventional slacks, but these are fashioned of the purest wool, fresh from the sheep. You may find it curious that at nine o'clock in the evening, it is wearing dark glasses. You may think it odd that the creature is wearing an ascot, for ascots rarely are seen in Wilkes-Barre, Pennsylvania.

When play of a board commences, it will be seen that this charming stranger has an uncanny way of becoming declarer in no trump contracts. The Little Old Lady seems positively to invite such a conclusion to the auction. On defense, the visitor makes the crushing lead. Others may finesse through East when the better path is through West, but the Professional Partner treads a surefooted way. At the conclusion of a hand, the stranger may offer a gentle suggestion having to do with watching its discards, but such suggestions always are preceded by, "My dear Gwendolyn."*

You will not be greatly surprised to learn a week or so later that Gwendolyn comes from Long Island, that Gwendolyn hungers for recognition as a Life Master, and that Gwendolyn has retained this smoothie for $500 a day and its tab at the Holiday Inn. Neither will you be amazed to learn that this interesting couple has finished first in the men's and women's KO teams and second in the masters.

---

*It does not call her Gwendolyn if her name is Janet. In private it may call her a good many other things.

The Double

Duplexis

FRANCIS and Truscott, in their authoritative *Official Encyclopedia of Bridge,* make a telling comment about the Double. The creature is identified in two broad classifications, the Penalty Double and the Takeout Double, and "distinguishing between the two types is not always easy."* Indeed this is not easy. Edwin B. Kantar verily has written: "Nowadays, when your partner doubles, only one person knows for sure what the double means—your partner."†

In the early days of auction bridge, the Informatory or Takeout Double had but one meaning: It signaled opening count and it said, "Partner, bid!" Partner might be holding a Yarborough. No matter. "Partner, bid!" As the Kingdom of Bridge expanded its domain, both the Takeout Double and the Penalty Double took on new configurations. By way of

---

*Fourth Edition, p. 114.

†I have forgotten where Kantar said this, probably in the ACBL Bulletin, but he said it. Kantar is a wise man.

example, imagine a familiar sequence of one heart by West, one spade by North, two hearts by East. South *doubles*. What does this mean? This evening that particular double is a Rosenkranz Double.‡ It means that South holds a top honor in spades and would like to go on a picnic.

In other times, places, and circumstances, scholars have recorded Negative Doubles (flocks of these), Responsive Doubles, Game-Try Doubles, Optionable Doubles, Rescue Doubles, the Sucker's Double, Lightner's Lead Directing Double,§ and even the Striped-Tail Ape Double.

This last creature, identified by John Lowenthal and Samuel Scaffidi, appears when North and South are fairly certain that East and West can make a small slam. At the level of four spades South doubles. An offended West redoubles, and South flees "like a striped-tail ape." West proceeds to make six and discovers that the score for four spades, doubled and redoubled, with two overtricks, is less than West could have scored by going to six. You should look it up.

As Professor Lorenz's illustration makes clear, the Double is always a peril for someone, either the doubler or the doubled. The cited spade hand could make only five. Takeouts of desperation can be disastrous. Sucker Doubles have a way of giving opponents top boards. Watch for thin ice and treat the Double with care. It is usually armed.

---

‡Named for Mr. Rosenkranz.
§Named for Mr. Lightner

The Jump Shift
Amphibia Transmuta

NORTH bids one heart. East passes. South bids two spades. *Zowie*! Look, daddy, a Jump Shift! And so it is, and no creature has a happier aspect.

Culbertson* generally is credited with identifying the Jump Shift, though it surely dates to the earliest days of whist. Culbertson called it the Jump Takeout or Forcing Takeout, but it is all the same thing. Its call is unmistakable: *Sub-lam, sub-lam*!† Its grand leaps bring a gasp from opponents and bring a sparkle to the eyes of the opening bidder.

In Culbertson's time, the aspects of the Jump Shift were universally described: nineteen points and a gorgeous suit, often by Hart, Shaffner & Marx. In recent years scholars have identified a number of variant sub-species. Sometimes it may indicate only sixteen or seventeen points; sometimes a Shift is bid with only three cards in the jumping suit. In one version‡ a

---

*Which see, p. 1.

†Robertson, op cit. p. 918.

‡A. Soloway.

Jump Shift may have three meanings: It could mean an all-wool suit of superior quality; it could mean a well-balanced wardrobe; or it could mean support for opener's suit, either by suspenders or by belt.

Another variant is more exotic.§ After an opening bid of one club, the Jump Shift leaps to two spades, which means a rock-solid holding in *diamonds*. That may fool everybody, including the opener, but it certainly adds excitement. In any version, the Jump Shift is a beautiful thing to behold. May it leap on forever! And may it land surely and solidly on the lily pad called Slam.

-----

§A. Passell-Strasburg.

The Opening Two

Maxima Arma Duo

To begin with, there are two Twos. One is weak, the other strong. The first has been raised on cream of wheat, skimmed milk, and egg custard. The other has been raised on honest meat and potatoes. You will note from the Plate opposite what a difference nutrition can make.

Vanderbilt* found the Weak Two in the forests of auction, gave it a couple of shots, fattened it with beef broth and good brandy, and gave it a new home in Contract. The Two then resembled the Preemptive Bid. Since then other scholars have identified Weak Twos in a different way. Much depends upon where the beast is sitting. Sitting south, after North and East have passed, a Weak Two may be a very weak sister indeed. In such situations, a seven-point rack of antlers is not unusual. Ordinarily Weak Twos are found with about eight to eleven

---

*Vanderbilt found all kinds of things in the shrubbery—Weak Twos, the Artificial Club Opener, the Negative One Diamond Response, seven McGregors and two Titleists.

high card points, most of the points being in a six-card suit. If the Weak Two has no six-card suit, it is not a Weak Two.

The Strong Two was identified by Culbertson† under the name of the Two Demand or Forcing Two. It is one of the relatively pure elements of the System that has survived the fading of Culbertson and the dawning of Goren. Generally this handsome and brawny beast carries from twenty-two to twenty-five points, which is often enough for game even if partner has a bust. Which partner ordinarily has.

In this event—the bust, that is to say—partner is required to speak to the rampant beast as follows: "Two no trump." That acts as an immediate depressant and has the effect of quieting the Strong Two. It then can be moved cautiously, if not actually to game, at least in the direction of game.

Other responses to the Strong Two are more positive. They encourage the beast to press on in the hope that a Slam may be just over the hill.

----

†Culbertson was no slouch at finding things himself.

The Slam

Elephas Maximus Septem (Minimus Sex)

I N the Bridge Battle of the Century 904 hands were dealt. Only one Grand Slam was bid, and on that one the Culbertson team went down. All told, thirty-one Little Slams were bid. The experts made seventeen of them and went down on fourteen.

The species clearly qualifies for classification, if not exactly as endangered, then certainly as rare. Like many rare collectibles, it is also valuable. Few experiences in an evening of money bridge are quite so satisfying as bringing home a Little Slam, vulnerable, doubled, in no trump. One can develop enduring affection for the beast.

The Slams are not especially interesting in themselves. Their aspects never change, and but two versions will ever be found: twelve tricks, Little; thirteen, Grand.

What is of more concern to investigators is the chase. Both the Little Slam and the Grand Slam may be pursued through the methods devised by Easley Blackwood in 1933 and refined by his successors. There is the basic Blackwood, in which North's bid of four no trump asks South, "Partner,

how many aces do you have?" South might as well say aloud, "two," but the Laws require that South say "five hearts." Now no one is in the dark about South's aces.

A livelier pursuit may be undertaken through the Byzantine Blackwood. It is properly named, for it involves such a maze of kings in key suits and kings in half-key suits that only the most experienced hunters can find their way. Another enjoyable pastime is to go after a Slam through the Roman Blackwood. Here a response of five diamonds could mean from one to four aces, and a response of five hearts could indicate two aces of the same color. Distantly related to the Roman Blackwood is the Black & Red Gerber. Here a Slam is sought by an asking bid of four clubs when a red suit has been agreed upon as the trump.

Not all searches involve a quest for aces. Such professional hunters as Lebovic inquire about singletons; Malowan asks about numbers of trumps. In San Francisco, where Slams are avidly pursued, a four no trump asking bid seeks information on aces (counted as three points) and kings (counted as one point). A response of five clubs, sad to say, shows less than three points; five diamonds, exactly three; five hearts, four; and so forth. Less precise, but more conversational, is the Declaratory-Interrogatory Exchange, in which North asks South, "Are you interested in going Slam hunting?" To which South replies, "Okay, unless there's something better on the tube."

Slam hunting is *always* better than staying home to watch the tube. It's riskier, too, but one who never hunts never brings home an *Elephas maximus septem*.

The No Trump

Trumpus Nullus

N o beast in the forests of Bridge is more admired by big game hunters than the No Trump. When the Grand Slam successfully is yoked to the No Trump, vulnerable, the hunter's happiness is supreme. Such a trophy rarely is seen, to be sure, but it is something to dream about.

Why is the No Trump so eagerly pursued? It is because of that beautiful forty-point score for the first trick. If a hunter brings home three No Trump, he has game worth putting on the table, with something left over for the freezer. For this reason, more hands are played in No Trump than in the suits.

Apart from its manifest strength, the creature's most endearing characteristic is its highly developed sense of curiosity. Often one will hear in the forest a call of "four No Trump?" The call requires translation. If one is speaking Blackwood, this means, "How many aces, partner?" The No Trump bid can have other translations also, depending upon whether one is speaking German, French, Hungarian, Roman,* Roth-

---

*Not to be confused with Italian.

Stone, or something that two partners have made up over a drink the night before. Sometimes a responsive call of "One No Trump" means "Sorry, pal, there ain't no game tonight." A responsive bid of two No Trump can be translated in at least six different ways. The literature contains references to a two No Trump response on six points and a six-five distribution. *This beast is dangerous.* From all of this we may conclude that few creatures are at once so versatile and so difficult to bring home as the long-horned species here depicted.

Many sub-species of the No Trump have been identified. Of particular interest is the Woodson No Trump.† Here we find that an opening one No Trump can mean *either* ten to twelve points *or* sixteen to eighteen points, and it is up to one's partner to find out by responding with two clubs. This may be translated as *combien, wie gehts, quelle heure est-il,* or *come off it.* Mention also should be made of the New Zealand Gladiator No Trump, in which a response of two diamonds means, "Let's run and play in the majors." People who are at home in diamonds always want to play in the majors. Yet another notable variant is the Dynamic No Trump, indicating an unbalanced, or slightly flaky fellow, who comes into view bearing eighteen to twenty-one points and a side saddle.

It remains to be said that in No Trump contracts, unlike suit contracts, one sets out by counting winners instead of losers. The bridge columnists, playing at the level of three, always deliver eight winners. It is up to the reader to bag the ninth.

---

†Named for Mr. Woodson.

The Precision Bids

Offerae Precisae

P RECISION Bids are not for everyone. *Chacun a son gout,* as the French say.* While most experts play Precision in some form, not all authorities commend it.†

Let us begin with an opening bid of one club. The response may be one diamond. This is known as the Impossible Negative‡ and shows a distribution of four/four/four/one. Over one diamond the opening bidder may respond with one heart, to which the responder replies three diamonds to show that the responder didn't have diamonds after all. This kind of thing is what makes the system so *precise,* because the opening bid of one club may have said nothing at all about clubs. There is also the Unusual Positive response, followed by Precision Asking Bids, followed by Super-Precision Asking Bids, followed by high winds and a 40 percent chance of rain.

Much of the Precision System was imported from Taiwan between 1970 and 1973. With constant practice and studious application, it can be mastered by anyone with an IQ of 460. Without such dedication, it can lead to spectacular tumbles.

---

* Champagne may cause gout.

†*Le Systeme de Precision: C'est pour Les Oiseaux;* M. Lamuela, Université de Paris Presse, 1976.

‡ So named for the girl who can't say no.

The Coup

Strokum Geniusi

THE Coup* is rare, the Coup is agile, the Coup is deceptive, and if one's certain trump trick is devoured by a Coup, the experience is altogether infuriating. Icthyologists have identified at least fifteen sub-species. All of them involve the use of legal traps, and all of them have very sharp teeth. Let us examine a few of these.

In the Grand Coup, the perpetrator deliberately ruffs a winning card. If the perpetrator ruffs two winning cards, he pulls off a Double Grand Coup. A Triple Grand Coup is more rare than a hat trick in hockey. The last known Triple was seen in the Sault Ste. Marie Grand Nationals of 1926.

The Bath Coup† involves the hold-up of an ace when one holds both the ace and the jack. This is a felony in eighteen states and the District of Columbia.

---

*Pronounced *coo,* as in bill and coup.

†Supposedly named for Bath, England, in the glorious days when much whist was played there. Other authorities say it comes from the despairing expostulation of a victim: "We sure took a bath on that one!"

The Coup en Passant, or two-door coup, promotes a low trump to a high trump. Such battlefield promotions are hard to come by and are therefore highly treasured.

Through the Deschapelles Coup,‡ one finds a way to get into partner's hand without breaking a window or picking the lock.

The Merrimac Coup requires the intentional sinking of a high card in order to knock out a vital entry in an opponent's hand.§

---

‡Alexandre Louis Honoré Lebreton Deschapelles (1780–1847) was a remarkable fellow. During a battle against English forces led by Horatio Hornblower, he lost his right hand to an English saber. He survived the wound and went on to become one of the great masters of whist in his time. Admiral Hornblower, a fine player himself, called him "an adversary always worthy of my steel." Deschapelles not only played one-handed whist; still more remarkably, he became a champion at billiards.

§Named for the *Merrimac,* a coal ship deliberately scuttled by the U.S. in Santiago Harbor in 1898 in an effort to bottle up the Spanish fleet. Not to be confused with the CSS *Merrimack,* aka the *Virginia,* which on March 7, 1862, fought an indecisive battle with the USS *Monitor.*

The Morton's Fork Coup offers defenders a profitless choice of taking a cheap trick now or losing a high trick later on.§§

We must also acknowledge the Coup en Blanc, or Duck Soup; the Devil's Coup, in which an opponent's trump trick is made to disappear before his very eyes, and the Scissors Coup, by which the opponents' communications are severed.

Finally we come to the Alcatraz Coup, described by Francis and Truscott as "a form of robbery that almost warrants a prison term for the perpetrator."§§§ This is not truly a Coup. It is an Impropriety of the grossest sort and ought never to be called a coup at all.

---

§§Named for John Cardinal Morton (1420–1500), a fighting prelate who joined Henry Tudor when Hank was still Earl of Richmond. After Henry killed Richard III at Bosworth Field, and thus became Henry VII, Morton became the king's chancellor of the exchequer. As such, according to Francis and Truscott (op.cit., p. 287), "he habitually extracted money from wealthy London merchants for the royal treasury." If a merchant lived ostentatiously, Morton would suggest that surely something could be spared for Henry; if the merchant lived frugally, then surely he had savings from which a contribution could be made. This was "Morton's Fork."

§§§Francis and Truscott provide an unspeakable example. The ace, jack and ten of hearts remain in Dummy. The king and three are in declarer's hand. Declarer, sitting south, pulls the jack from the Dummy. East plays a small card. South then *fails to follow suit.* West produces either the queen or a small card. If it is a small card, South promptly corrects his revoke by playing the three; if it is the queen, South corrects his revoke by playing his king "and sweetly permitting West to change his play." The next call is for "Director!" and the call after that is for whips and hunting hounds to drive the scoundrel from the floor.

The Impropriety

Goofus Major

THE Impropriety appears in many guises. None of them is in any way admirable. The most familiar of these is the Coffee House Impropriety. "I see you're wearing your diamond tonight," says wily Willie, sitting south, to sly Selma sitting north. Whereupon Selma leads—a diamond. What else? "These square hands are killing me," says Willie, who holds a singleton club and a void in spades.

The Impropriety has no manners; it has no couth. It will hash loudly and lengthily over a hand that has just been played, thereby delaying the entire room. It will sneak a peak into an opponent's hand at the slightest opportunity. It will howl indignantly against the least hesitation by an opponent—but not so indignantly that the Director will be summoned. The Impropriety will drum its fingers impatiently while the opposition is pondering a bid or a play. It will make a distracting hum. It will smoke in the presence of nonsmoking opponents. These are the Obnoxious Improprieties.

The most despicable Impropriety is the flat-out cheat.

These are among the rarest of all creatures in the Kingdom of Bridge. From time to time, charges of cheating are brought: at Buenos Aires in 1965, it was alleged that a British team used fingers to signal information. At Bermuda in 1975, it was charged that two Italians communicated by foot signals beneath the table. In other incidents, Improprieties have involved signals by scoring pencil (position of the eraser), by cigarettes (lit or held in a particular way), and by the blowing of one's nose at a critical time. Such Improprieties do not walk, fly, swim, or crawl. They slink. Extermination is the approved treatment.

The Laydown
Signum Victorae

T HE Laydown, known in Arkansas and east Texas as the Pianola, is a generally friendly and amiable creature. It appears most often after trumps have been pulled, wearing a confident smile and a neat straw hat. "The board is cold," says declarer. "It's a Laydown," declarer adds, and spreads his hand.

Nine times out of ten, the complacent declarer is exactly right. No defense will defeat the contract. But now and then the Laydown proves not to be a Laydown at all. It is an Upstart Laydown. No sooner has the hand been spread by South than East announces a Lead that will reduce this happy cat to a state of total disarray.

Laydowns thus should be regarded with affection mixed with two tablespoons of suspicion. They should be inspected closely for fleas. If the animal is found to be in good health and spirits, nothing remains to be said by opponents but *deal*!